Make Full Proof of Your Ministry

A GUIDEBOOK
TO EMPOWER THE 21ST CENTURY EVANGELIST

Evangelist Diane L. North

Regional Elect-Lady ♦ Region #2

"The Flame of Evangelism Must Never Go Out"

It's all about Souls !

ISBN 13: 978-0-615-14664-5

First printing   May 2007

The Author is available to present this material upon request through Seminars and Conferences. Scheduling and availability information may be obtained via Publicist using the contact information below.

Additional copies of this book are available by mail. Send $20.00 plus $3.00 for shipping and handling to:

Evangelist Diane L. North
P. O. Box 300095
Kansas City, MO 64130
(816) 419-0111
Email: evangelist@dianenorthministries.org
Website: www.dianenorthministries.org

Printing in the U.S.A.
Morris Publishing
3212 East Highway 30
Kearney, NE 68847
1-800-650-7888

TABLE OF CONTENTS

~ About the Author ~

FOREWORD

After reviewing this Guidebook, it is my opinion that all who are called to the office of Evangelism will greatly benefit from the material contained herein. This tremendous body of work will be an asset to any library and a valuable tool for winning souls for the body of Christ.

I appreciate the work of Evangelist Diane North on this book, showing her passion and love for lost souls. She gives clear direction and methods for reaching the lost.

This book is a "must read" and not one that you will simply throw on the bookshelf and forget. The timeless information will help you stay on the cutting edge of Evangelism. The reference material contained herein will equip you to reach out into your communities and change them for Christ. This book contains easy to read language that will provide solid guidance on the Do's and Don'ts of Evangelism. You will gain a deeper knowledge of your calling with this material and be prepared to teach others on Local, District, Jurisdictional and National levels.

Reading this book you will explore many key areas of Evangelism and their respective areas of responsibility. If you are reading this foreword, it is because you have made one of the best investments in preparing yourself for the task to which God has called you.

President Dennis L. Martin, Sr.
International Department of Evangelism
Church of God in Christ, Inc.

ACKNOWLEDGEMENT

One thing I know for sure, when God births something in you, an idea, a dream or even a passion, He will take full responsibility to make it happen, if you just let Him.

I would first like to thank God, for putting a love for souls in my sprit. To the following people I would like to say thank you for your time and support. It would not have been possible to complete this Guidebook without your help. May God's blessing rest upon each of you.

- To my Mother, Dr. Pearl Green who provided early training, direction and instruction throughout my life. Thank you for the opportunity for hosting my seminar at your church and encouraging me to include that material in this Guidebook.
- To my Pastor/Friend, Superintendent Frank Douglas, Jr. thank you for your professional and personal support you shared with me over the years. With your love and encouragement I'm able to trust God for my next assignment.
- To my first Editor, Linda Milan, M.Div. thanks for taking time while working on your Master of Divinity to review, make corrections and discuss the book with me.
- To my typist, Judy Diamond, I sincerely appreciate how you patiently worked with me over the past 90 days making corrections, meeting with me weekly and seeing that this book took on a professional tone.
- To my Sister, Crystal Young, friend and confidante, thanks for coming to see about me during a challenging time in my life and taking out time to assist in reviewing and formatting my Guidebook.
- To my friend and cover page designer, Beverly Fuqua, thank you for your creative work with the front cover of my Guidebook, thanks and many more thanks for your assistance while recovering from back surgery.
- To my newest friend and Computer Engineer, Marty Beaugard I'm indebted to you for your weekly support and assistance with all of my technical needs, and thanks for your expertise in designing my webpage, assisting me with my domain name and email address.
- To Missionary Icy Gines, a noted author and writer, a dear friend of mine for over 40 years, thanks for taking out the time to assist and provide direction through the processes of having a book prepared for publishing.
- To Pastor Fred Gibbs, my Assistant Pastor, friend and master teacher, thank you for your final editing and sharp eye for perfecting the contents and context of my Guidebook. And thank you Jeannine for making this possible.
- To Elder Dennis Martin, Sr., International President of the Department of Evangelism, I sincerely appreciate you taking the time to review this material and provide me with a heartfelt Foreword.

If I can see further than other men,
it is because I have stood on the shoulders of Giants.

DEDICATION

This Guidebook is dedicated to men and women that have accepted the call of God to "Go into all the world". Whether that call is in our homes, down the street or in some foreign Country. Evangelist that have counted up the cost and yield their ears to the voice of God. This book is for Evangelists that have a genuine burden for lost souls. Evangelist that will not rest until they have prepared, equipped and empowered themselves to face the challenges of the 21st Century.

Evangelist, We've Gotta Job to Do!!

Three scriptures I want all Evangelist to embrace:

Behold, I give unto you power to tread on serpents and scorpions, and over all the power Of the enemy: and nothing shall by any means hurt you. Luke 10:19

Who shall separate us from the love of Christ? Shall tribulation, or distress, or persecution, or famine, or nakedness, or peril, or sword? Romans 8:35

What shall we then say to these things? If God be for us, who can be against us? Romans 8:31

Evangelist Diane L. North

PREFACE

Evangelism is tracts, crusades, and altar calls. It's door-to-door witnessing. Weekly night visitations, revivals.

At least, that's what we often assume.

Actually, Evangelism is much broader than those techniques......much bigger than a once-a-year event or a weekly program. It's both natural and supernatural. It's as complex as the relationships it flows out of and as diverse as the people it reaches. The gospel proclaims that Evangelism is God's channel of love to a lost and needy world.

I'm so glad you've taken the time to take a fresh look at Evangelism with me. I promise you, this won't be a *"ten steps to successful soul winning"* type book. As helpful as good techniques are, I've decided to focus this book on relationship, attitudes, lifestyles, and perspectives ---- the heart of the Believer. Because that's where true Evangelism begins.

We have been given a mission and a mandate from God, and we can only fulfill it when we experience unrest regarding the condition of lost souls.

It is easy to be dressed up with fancy clothes, but it is work to visit the nursing homes, the prisons, the sick in the hospital, the troubled teens, the drug addicts and alcoholics in the community.

Just like the world needed Jesus yesterday, the world need us today. We must go out to where people are. Our churches, seminars and conventions are for equipping and preparing us for lost souls. Then we are ready to meet every challenge.

Evangelist, how much are you willing to sacrifice for a dying community? Are you willing to push back the plate? Turn off CSI, Law and Order, American Idol and many other television sitcoms that eat up our time? There are lost souls waiting for you and me to impart into their lives, the message that Jesus loves them.

During this end time we must step up our game plan. If we have prayed two times a week for fifteen minutes, it is of urgent matter that we pray every day fifteen minutes and more.

Evangelist, it is only when we have, "Prayed the Price" that we will get results. And if we want a mighty breakthrough and strongholds to be broken, we are going to have to fast.

Remember, what the disciples said to Jesus. *"Why couldn't we cast out him out". Jesus answered and said, "because of your unbelief: for verily I say unto you, If ye have faith as a grain of mustard seed, ye shall say unto this mountain, remove hence to yonder place; and it shall remove; and nothing shall be impossible unto you. Howbeit this kind goeth not out but by prayer and fasting". Matt. 17:19-21*

Evangelist, we must understand that we only have twenty-four hours in a day and we have been encouraged to work while it is day. *I must work the works of him that sent me, while it is day: the night cometh, when no man can work.* John 9:4

Lastly, a solemn warning has been given to each of us and we must take it seriously, "*But as the days of Noah were, so shall also the coming of the Son of man be. For as in the days that were before the flood they were eating and drinking, marrying and giving in marriage, until the day that Noah entered into the ark, and knew not until the flood came, and took then all away; so shall also the coming of the Son of man be*". Matt. 24:37-29

I encourage each Evangelist and those inspired to become evangelist as you read the pages of this book to get back on the firing line to do what you were called to do.

GO AND MAKE DISCIPLES!!

Ask God to put a burning desire for lost souls in your spirit. Commit to this great work--- understanding that prisons are filling up daily. Women are going to prison at an alarmingly faster rate than men. AIDS in the black community has sky rocketed. Homosexuality has become a common place on the television networks.

Evangelist, if we don't go who will?

"We've Gotta Job To Do"!!!!

INTRODUCTION

<u>EVANGELISM</u>

Souls cannot be saved and no revival winds can blow without the presence and work of the Holy Spirit.

The aim of Evangelism is to confront the world with the Gospel of Christ. We believe, and teach that, we must make sure our Evangelism does not draw upon "a bag of clever tricks." Our Evangelism must draw upon the very truth by which the Church lives, moves, and has its being. We must slay all tricks, traps and techniques which has and will cheapen Evangelism.

The Evangelism that stops with saving the soul and does not go on to build Christian character is inadequate. Evangelism's greatest failure is found in the fact that many converts do not stand. They soon fade from the picture, because their knowledge of the faith is so inadequate. Evangelism's chief problem is to "hold" its converts and enlist them in the total ministry of the church. Christian character is a basic essential….The only way to build Christian character is through a steady diet of the strong meat of the Word. A thorough spiritual diet of doctrinal instruction can grow strong bones and muscles of Christian character.

<u>A FAITHFUL EVANGELIST</u>

➢ **Has a Hunger for God's Word:**

"As newborn babes, desire the sincere milk of the word, that ye may grow thereby". (I Peter 2:2)

➢ **Has a Thirst For Holy Living:**

"And hereby we do know that we know him, if we keep his commandments". (Psalms 63:1)

➢ **Has a Desire for Greater Knowledge of God:**

"As the hart panteth after the water brooks, so panteth my soul after thee." (Psalms 42:1)

➢ **Has a Desire to be used by God:**

"For I long to see you, that I may impart unto you some spiritual gifts, to the end ye may be established." (Roman 1:11)

➢ **Has a Love for People:**

"A new commandment I give unto you. That ye love one another; as I have loved you, that ye also love one another". (John 13:34)

The " Mission" of the Church

Through sound teaching we know that the Church is *not* an *"Organization"* but an *"Organism."* Therefore it is not a *"Social Club,"* organized and supported solely for the benefit of its members. It is not a *"Place of Amusement"* to ponder to the carnal nature of man. It is not a *"House of Merchandise"* for the sale of *"Indulgences"* or other commodities, whereby the money of the ungodly can be secured to save the penurious church member a little self sacrifice. Neither is it a *"Reform Bureau"* to save the "bodies" of men. The reformation of men is very commendable, as are all forms of *"Social Service,"* but that is not the work or mission of the Church.

In the days of Christ, the world was undoubtedly faced with the same degree of evil doings facing our current society. Perhaps, even to a greater degree, nevertheless, neither Christ nor his Apostles organized any reform agency. He knew that the source of all the evils in the world is SIN, and the only way to eradicate sin is to Regenerate the Human Heart, and so he gave to the world the GOSPEL, and the Mission of the Church is to carry that Gospel to the Whole World. *Mark 16:15* The Gospel is not a system of "Ethics," or a "Code of Morals," it is a :

Proclamation of Salvation

For I am not ashamed of the gospel of Christ:
for it is the power of God unto salvation to every one that believeth;
to the Jew first, and also to the Greek.
--Romans 1:16

The purpose of the Gospel in this dispensation is not to *"Save Society,"* but to *"Save the Individual Members of Society"* that are to compose the "Body of Christ" – THE CHURCH.

In this dispensation the great mistake the Church has made is in appropriating to herself, in this Dispensation, the promises of earthly conquest and glory, which belong exclusively to Israel in the Millennial, or "Kingdom Age." As soon as the Church enters unto an "Alliance with the World," and seeks the help of Parliaments, Congresses, Legislatures, Federations and Reform Societies, largely made up of ungodly men and women, she loses her spiritual power and becomes helpless as a redeeming force.[1]

---

[1]Clarence Larkin, <u>Dispensational Truth</u> (Pennsylvania: Rev. Clarence Larken, 1918) p. 78

Chapter 1

Evangelism

- ❖ **Mandate For Today**

- ❖ **Make Full Proof of your Ministry**

- ❖ **The Work of An Evangelist**

- ❖ **The Ministry of the Evangelist**

- ❖ **Mission Statement for the Evangelist**

MANDATE FOR TODAY

Every generation moving into Christian responsibility and leadership should rethink evangelism. Though the message does not change and the gospel is always current, it is helpful to re-evaluate the methods of evangelism utilized by church educational agencies to be sure the proclamation of Christ is being heard.

Each new generation of Christians must communicate the gospel to its peers. Methods or techniques used to do this must take into consideration contemporary society and its values. Those who would share Christ must understand the people around them and clearly relate to them.

New evangelism methods often are efficient and winsome ways to witness effectively. During recent years Evangelism has received new emphasis through attractive Christian literature, beach evangelism, home and professional Bible classes, camping and campus ministry. Both time-tested methods and fresh new ways should be used to share the gospel at all age levels.

Evangelism through Christian education is the mandate for church growth today. Both numerical and spiritual growth result from Evangelism in the church educational program. Without Evangelism, the educational program becomes routine and unproductive.

Christian education and Evangelism compliment each other. Christ was teacher and evangelist. Those who would follow him cannot separate the two ministries. Opportunities for Evangelism in local church educational agencies are many. Added to these are opportunities for personal Evangelism by teachers and educational leaders who love the Lord. It cannot be ignored. Evangelism is not an elective. It is a divine imperative which every believer should obey.

One of the greatest dangers facing the church in Evangelism is the lack of concern, and active involvement in touching the lives of others who are without Christ.

Revitalizing Evangelism must be evidenced in church educational programs which will transform Christians into active soul winners. Those engaged in church education have a divine challenge to evangelize.

MAKE FULL PROOF OF YOUR MINISTRY

Do you know what your ministry is?

Having then gifts differing according to the grace that is given to us, whether prophecy, let us prophesy according to the proportion of faith; or ministry, let us wait on our ministry, or he that teacheth, on teaching. Romans 12:6-7

One that has made full proof of his/her ministry has accomplished, carry out, performed that which God has given them to do.

I charge thee therefore before God, and the Lord Jesus Christ, who shall judge the quick and the dead at his appearing and his kingdom; preach the word, be instant in season, out of season, reprove, rebuke, exhort with all longsuffering and doctrine. For the time will come when they will not endure sound doctrine, but after their own lusts shall they heap to themselves teachers, having itching ears; and they shall turn away their ears from the truth, and shall be turned unto fables. But watch thou in all things, endure afflictions, do the work of an evangelist, make full proof of thy ministry. II Timothy 4:1-5

Here Paul expresses great seriousness and earnestness as he presses Timothy to the diligent discharge of his work and office as an Evangelist. All gospel ministers are to take on the charge given to Timothy. Why must Timothy now be instant in season, and out of season? Paul knew his time was running out. There was urgency with his message to young Timothy. The seasoned warrior was about to leave the scene and wanted the young Evangelist to be ready. Evangelist, how serious have you taken your call from God?

Paul's ministry was not just a matter of choice or personal ambition. It was something he was called to do. He did not just have "preacher's itch". He was called to preach and bound to fulfill that call.

For though I preach the gospel, I have nothing to glory of; for necessity is laid upon me; yea woe is unto me, if I preach not the gospel! I Corinthians 9:16

Paul's final testimony to Timothy. A solemn charge. Preach the Word!

Many Evangelists preach their ideas, their opinion, some count their experience as Gospel. But Paul instructed Timothy to Preach the Word! As a pastor, Timothy was not required to merely know the word or like the word or approved of the word; he was required to preach the word. The word of God must be preached by Timothy. It was to be the content of his message.

Why must the word be preached? Because it is the infallible Word of God that will change man. It is the Word of God that can change a life of sin to a life pleasing to God. One God's word can heal a dying home, dying community, dying world. Without the preached Word, we would all die in our sins.

Not everyone who opens a Bible and starts talking is preaching the word. Many well-intentioned Evangelists are actually preaching themselves instead of the Gospel. If the focus is on the funny stories, jokes, our failures and accomplishments, we are preaching not Christ but ourselves. And this is what Paul instructed Timothy to do.

Evangelist we must always be ready, in season and out of season. We should preach the Gospel when it is easy and preach it when it is hard. We should preach it when the fruit is evident and preach it when the fruit seems invisible.

There was once a Church of England clergyman who was gloriously saved. When Jesus changed his life he started preaching the Gospel to his whole parish and they all got saved. Then he started preaching in neighboring parishes, and the clergymen of those parishes were offended. They asked the Bishop to make the man stop. When the Bishop confronted him he said, "I hear you are always preaching and you don't seem to be doing anything else". The changed man answered, "Well Bishop, I only preach during two seasons of the year". The Bishop said, "I'm glad to know that, what seasons are they"? He replied, "In season and out of season".

The Apostle Paul encouraged Timothy to convince, rebuke, exhort, with all longsuffering and teaching. In his preaching Timothy was to bring the Word of God to bear on the lives of his people. He was not to treat the word as if it were filled with interesting ideas or fascinating theories that did not produce life changing results. He was to hold up the Word of God against the lives of his people and let God do his work.

For the time will come when they will not endure sound doctrine, but according to their own desires, because they have itching ears, they will heap up for themselves teachers, and they will turn their ears away from the truth, and be turned aside to fables. They will not endure sound doctrine. Timothy needed to keep focused on the Word of God because man, by his natural instinct, does not want God's revelation. He would rather hear what he wants to hear. Something to scratch his itching ears.

For the time will come when they will not endure sound doctrine; but after their own lust shall heap to themselves teachers, having itching ears. II Timothy 4:3 Once people leave the Word of God they often then embrace fantastic fantasies. When a man rejects God's truth, it isn't that he believes in nothing, he will believe in anything. It is possible for many church goers to turn aside from the truth and to believe many fables.

The fable that you must earn your way before God.
The fable that God only loves you when you are good.
The fable that you should walk around thing of yourself as better than other because your are a Christian.

But watch thou in all things, endure afflictions, do the work of an Evangelist, make full proof of they ministry. I Timothy 4:5

The more determined men become to despise the teachings of Christ, the more zealous godly ministers should be to assert it and the more strenuous their efforts to preserve it. Timothy could not fulfill his ministry unless he kept careful attention, being watchful in all things. Every good Evangelist has his/her eyes open.

Endure afflictions. Ministry is just like life. There are afflictions to be borne with. For some this is a disturbing thought because they thought that the ministry would be one beautiful spiritual experience after another. There are plenty of wonderful blessings in serving God, but there are also afflictions to be endured.

Do the work of an Evangelist. This implies that Timothy was not particularly gifted as an Evangelist, but he still had to faithfully do that work as a preacher of God's Word. Fulfill your ministry. Paul worked to it's completion. We are to leave nothing undone, work out our ministry. Don't start good and give up after a few bumps, complete the assignment. Evangelist we do not retire!

There may be many reasons why the Evangelist's Ministry goes unfulfilled. The following must be battled daily:

- Fear
- Unbelief
- The cares of the world
- The fear of man
- Criticism and discouragement
- Besetting sin

Paul conclude with these final words:

For I am now ready to be offered, and the time of my departure is at hand. I have fought a good fight, I have finished [my] course, I have kept the faith; Henceforth there is laid up for me a crown of righteousness, which the Lord, the righteous judge, shall give me at that day, and not to me only, but unto all them also that love his appearing. Do thy diligence to come shortly unto me. II Timothy 4:6-9.

THE WORK OF AN EVANGELIST

This material is designed to meet our culture. Many groups have literature that speaks on Evangelism, but is not meeting the need with clear direction how to go out to a dying world.

I pray that the information that is in this book encourages you to work in your local Jurisdiction and Churches.

Many see the work of an Evangelist as a glamorous job. We have seen the traveling Evangelist come to town with many glitzy television presentations. Evangelism is more than that. We never know where we might be called out by God to <u>GO</u>. A hospital, a jail, a nursing home, to foreign lands. A good example would be, Philip in the desert; we have read how Philip had preached to the multitudes and the people gave heed to the things he spake. For unclean spirits, crying with loud voice, came out of many that were possessed with them: and many taken with palsy, and they that were lame, were healed. Philip did not object to leaving the great successful work in Samaria to go out to the desolate desert, for one moment.

When you look at the word "work" this implies a task to be undertaken, bodily and mental activity, to cause to toil, and labor. The secular world takes time to send employees to extensive training to learn the ins and outs of their job. They realize that the company can be no greater than its employees. Most companies need competent employees to meet the demand of the competitive environment that we are in today. The world of Evangelist should be no less prepared.

Question: How much time are you allowing God to train you for this work? Before Uncle Sam (Armed Forces) sends soldiers out to combat they are put through days and nights of critical and rigorous training. For what purpose? To test their strength and ability to meet the enemy head on.

Question: How can we as Evangelist be effective going out into a dark, cold, hateful world? When men, women and children defy the God we serve, when men's hearts have turned from God to do as they please. What motivates us as Evangelist to stay on the cutting edge and not give in or give up telling our life changing story? *(That Jesus came to save all sinners).*

- Are you making yourself available to be trained for these times?
- Have you updated your methods (techniques, processes, systems, means, manners, routines, approaches that were in place.)
- Are you still using the same methods that was in place 10, 20 30, or 40 years ago?
- Do we expect to be viable (useful) during this end time?

Then we must have:

- Strategy – idea, proposal, design
- Plan – preparation, training, research, groundwork

We must have methods that are:

- Current ; present, existing, in progress, recent, up-to-date and modern
- Relevant – pertinent, significant, important, to-the-point
- In touch – informed, involved, connected, in turn, knowledgeable, well-versed, learned, educated, instep, on the same wavelength, well-informed, on the ball, on top of things.

Then we must have a strategy (idea, proposal, design). We must have a plan (preparation, training, research, groundwork). We must have methods that are current (present, existing, in progress, recent, up-to-date and modern), relevant (pertinent, significant, important, to the point) and in touch (informed, involved, connected, in tune, clued-up knowledgeable, well-versed, learned, educated, concerned, linked, instep, on the same wavelength, well-informed, on the ball, on top of things).

Evangelist, this seems to be an overwhelming responsibility, but if we are to go out and be effective, we dare not find ourselves without proper training, and equipping ourselves on a daily basis. If we do not prepare ourselves adequately, the blood of lost souls will be required on our hands.

THE MINISTRY OF THE EVANGELIST

I. **Divine Call**

    A.   You do not enter the ministry as an Evangelist just because you feel like it.

        1.   You cannot make yourself an Evangelist.

        2.   It is dangerous to do something just because you want to.

        3.   You do not attempt to become an Evangelist just because someone else tells you that you can do it.

    B.   How does one know he/she is called to be an Evangelist?

        1.   You will have a conviction in your Spirit.

        2.   You will have the witness in your heart.

        3.   God will give you gifts that go along with the office to which you are called.

        4.   When a person is called to the ministry, there is an anointing that comes upon them, enabling them to stand in that office.

II. **Development, Maturity, Growth**

The word "Evangelist" refers to a person authorized to proclaim the gospel of Christ. It means "One Who Proclaims Good Tidings" *Ephesians 4:11*; *II Timothy 4:5*.

The Evangelist was a gift of God to the Church (*Ephesians 4:11*). These persons traveled over a wide geographical area, preaching as led by the Holy Spirit.

    A.   The ministry of the Evangelist must be developed. If you are called as an evangelist, it takes time to develop your ministry. Read *Romans 12:6-7*. Wait on our ministry.

    B.   God just equips you, and you must mature naturally and spiritually.

    C.   Philip started out in the ministry of helps (*Acts 6:1-6*). He was faithful in that office. Later he was moved to the office of the Evangelist (*Acts 8:5-7; 2:8*).

    D.   God may have called you to be an Evangelist. You may someday preach to 3,000. However, you won't start out preaching to 3,000. You may begin by preaching to 3, 5, or 10.

E.   Seek spiritual growth and development with your ministry before you identify and publish your ministry.

F.   Do not despise the day of small things (*Zechariah 4:10*)

III.   The Ministry of the Evangelist

Soul winning is a mandate from God. It is not an option, but a command. Consider *Mark 16:15-16.* *"And he said unto them, Go ye into all the world, and preach the gospel to every creature. He that believeth and is baptized shall be saved; but he that believeth not shall be damned"*.

A.   The Ministry of the Evangelist is to win men and women to Christ.

B.   The Ministry of the Evangelist is to continually remind us of the lost and dying world and its need for the gospel.

C.   The Ministry of the Evangelist is to go and help the pastor of the church where he/she is running revival.

Soul winning is a mandate from God. It is not an option, but a command. Consider *Mark 16:15-16.* *"And he said unto them, Go ye into all the world, and preach the gospel to every creature. He that believeth and is baptized shall be saved; but he that believeth not shall be damned"*.

Motto
"It's All About Souls"

"One Can Put A Thousand To Flight;
Two Can Put Ten Thousand To Flight"

Ephesians 4:11-15

And He gave some apostles; and some prophets; and some pastors and teachers; for the perfecting of the saints, for the work of the ministry, for the edifying of the body of Christ.

Till we all come in the unity of the faith, and of the knowledge of the Son of God, unto a perfect man, unto the measure of the statue of the fullness of Christ.

That we henceforth be no more children, tossed to and fro, and carried about with every wind of doctrine, by the sleight of men, and cunning craftiness, whereby they lie in wait to deceive;

But speaking the truth in love, may grow up into him in all things, which is the head, even Christ.

Mission Statement

Our Mission is to be instruments lead by the Holy Spirit in bringing unity, restoration and renewal to the Families, Communities, Churches and aboard.

Our goal is to refresh and rekindle the hearts and minds of the members throughout our local body that we may all receive the fullness of God's blessings.

Our Mission is to raise the consciousness of believer's to come to the knowledge and understanding of what God is doing through the Holy Spirit during these last days.

Our goal is to point members of our churches to the scriptures, which allows us to become steadfast and unmovable, and always able to stand and withstand against the wiles of the devil.

Our Mission is to provide instruction and guidance through the Word of God. We also intend to provide spiritual leadership to others. That we, along with our local members, may become complete, capable and proficient in the knowledge of Jesus Christ.

Our goal is to be a department that is persistent in prayer, for our Families, our Communities, our Churches, our District, our Jurisdiction and our national Church.

Our Mission is to teach believers to maintain their composure in the face of difficulties. Teaching other believers they must be ready to endure hardship as a good soldier as the pressure mounts.

Our goal is to develop believers to become totally reliable on the inspired infallible written Word of God. Stressing the importance of daily study and meditation, with awareness that knowing God brings eternal life.

Lastly, our Mission is to direct believers to look to Jesus as the primary source for comfort, guidance and hope on a day-to-day basis, committed first to our homes and then reaching out.

The chief mission of the Evangelist is: "To proclaim the gospel at every opportunity in season and out of season.

Chapter 2

A PRESENTATION FOR THE EVANGELIST ON THE MOVE

ARE YOU MAKING THE BEST OF YOUR TIME?

❖ A Time for Every Purpose

❖ Time is of the Essence

❖ Time Management

A TIME FOR EVERY PURPOSE

Ecclesiastes 3:1-8

To everything there is a season and a time to every purpose under heaven:

a time to be born, and a time to die;

a time to plant, and a time to pluck up that which is planted;

a time to kill, and a time to heal;

a time to break down, and a time to build up;

a time to weep, and a time to laugh;

a time to mourn, and a time to dance;

a time to cast away stones together, and a time to gather stones;

a time to embrace, and a time to refrain from embracing;

a time to get, and a time to lose;

a time to keep, and a time to cast away;

a time to rend, and a time to sew;

a time to keep silence, and a time to speak;

a time to love, and a time to hate; a time of war, and a time of peace.

TIME IS OF THE ESSENCE

"Does thou Love Life"? Then do not squander time. Time is the stuff life is made of.

We don't feel time, we don't hear time, we don't see time, if just quickly passes by us.

Everyone wants more time. Time to work, to play, to give, to experience, to live.

I will share with you profound insights that unlock personal energies for achievement, helpful remedies of your hidden potential and proven time management techniques that will put you on the cutting edge.

Let's start by gaining a unique look at the mysteries of time. Understanding how and why ancient cultures struggled with productivity and sought ways to lengthen the day.

You will learn to build your productivity pyramid starting with your personal "governing values" as a base, than moving upward using powerful goal planning ideas that lead to real day-to-day achievement.

How many struggle with procrastination, multiple interruptions, or conflicting priorities? We will discover effective principles that will help us have control over these universal time robbers.

We will talk about the importance of working with other people, with an emphasis on delegation and tools that will make you a master of follow-up.

These tools we will learn about have become indispensable tools for thousands.

Scheduling Your Time

If you control your time, you control your life.

Time is a precious commodity, everyone gets an equal share but we use it very differently.

The idea is to decide "what is the best use of my time? Make a list of what you need to do each week and then, based on the time available, make a daily "to-be-done-list" for working on your high priority tasks.

Purpose: To make better use of your time, both in terms of devoting time to high priority and avoiding wasting time or spending your time on less important things.

Step 1:   **Set your priorities.** List your major goals for the next few months. Rate each goal. Ask, "What are the most important things for me to do"?

Step 2:   **List what needs to be done this week** in order to reach your top priority goals. Rate each activity.

Step 3:   **Observe how you spend your time**. Each of us has 168 hours in a week.

Step 4:   **Make a master schedule of fixed activities for the week.** Time with God, sleeping, dressing, eating, meetings, classes, housekeeping, time with children, family, friends, leisure time, relaxation, exercise time.

Step 5:   **Keep a running list of assignments.** – things you need to get done this week.

Step 6:   **Make a "To-be-done-list" for every day.**

Do scheduling early in the day or at night before bed time. Try at the same time to make it a habit. It takes 21 days before a certain thing we do becomes a habit. **Whether it is good or bad.**

We are indebted to an anonymous poet for the following words of truth about the marvelous effect of habits.

I am your companion. I am your greatest Helper or heaviest burden.

I will push you onward or drag you down to failure. I am completely at your command.

Half the things you do you might just as well turn over to Me and I will do them-----quickly and correctly.

I am easily managed---you must merely be firm with me. Show me exactly how you want something done and after a few lessons I will do it automatically.

I am the servant of all great people; and, alas, of all failures as well.

Those who are great, I have made great. Those who are failures, I have made failures.

I am not a machine, though I work with all the precision of a machine, plus the intelligence of a person.

You may run me for profit or run me for ruin---it makes no difference to me.

Take me, train me, be firm with me, and I will place the world at your feet.

Be easy with me and I will destroy you. Who am I?

I Am Habit!

Don't use your peak performance time for easy assignments or for socializing and playing.

You must identify if you are a morning person or night person. To identify which will allow you to do your best work.

Step 7:   **Follow your daily to-be-done list.** Definitely reward yourself.

Basic Point: Work on your highest priority activities during most of your "free" time each day. Many of us procrastinate when faced with long and difficult or unpleasant tasks, even though they are quite important to us.

What are the solutions?

The best is to "recognize" the tendency to "put it off" and, instead, do it now!

Recognize that putting off an inevitable chore just generates more stress and embarrassment.

16

Since you will begin to see the reward in what you do, make a point throughout the day to reward yourself. Give yourself a 15 minute break; go out for a walk down the street and back. Sit back and put your feet up and close your eyes. Just take a breather.

Do you see a need for a schedule yet?

Maybe your memory is as sharp as it was 20 years ago; maybe your responsibility in the Ministry with your spouse is minimum, maybe you have gotten tired and say within yourself, "I'll leave it up to them".

Last note on this section:

Don't make your daily schedule too rigid and overly demanding. Your schedule should make you feel as if you've "got it all together" not like a failure or incompetent.

One of the vital principles of effective time management is learning to adapt when we face events which are beyond our control.

Much of the stress we experience in our lives is a result of inappropriate responses and, failure to adapt to events.

Time management presented here goes far beyond the list making and prioritizing.

Personal organizers and planners do not work in isolation. I don't know of one person who suddenly became organized and more efficient because he or she bought an organizer. You must develop the self-discipline to use the system as intended, whether that is to make notes while talking on the telephone or scheduling your major tasks in the planner or jotting down assignments and other information as they occur In other words, you must power the system in order for it to work.

Most time management systems come with instructions on how to use the system. But they fail to explain that you have to develop new habits in order to make them work.

It's encouraging to realize that a good habit is just as hard to break as a bad habit. Once you have formed new habits, you are unlikely to slip back to your old ways. The habits must be firmly entrenched. Don't rush the process. Form one habit at a time. One new habit each month will produce a major change in your operating methods within a few years.

If you are unwilling to commit the time and energy needed to make a time management system work, don't waste money buying one. Disorganization is not illegal. And it never killed anyone. At least not right away.

If you fail to control the events in your life, then events in your life will control you.

Planning

The key to Control: IF YOU FAIL TO PLAN, YOU PLAN TO FAIL!

How many more years do you expect to live?

We can waste our money and we're only out of money, but when we waste our time we have lost a portion of our life.

If planning is the key to control, why is it so many of us ignore it?

1.   I already know what I have to do. Why take the time to plan.
2.   Planning doesn't work for me, I have too many interruptions.
3.   I feel "tied down" when I have a long list of things I have to do.
4.   I don't have time to plan.
5.   I don't know how to plan properly.

Note: We must take time to sharpen the saw.

The more rushed we are, the more time we better spend planning our time and actions.

Goals and Goal Setting

If you really know what things you want out of life, it's amazing how opportunities will come to enable you to carry them out.

Someone has said, that a goal is "a dream with a deadline".

Serious goal setting produces serious results!

The Power in Today

A successful life does not result from chance nor it is determined by fate or good fortune, but from a succession of successful days.

Most organized people will use, on a daily basis, several devices to help them stay "organized".

These would probably include:
An appointment book
A daily "to-do-list"
A pad for daily notes
A phone/address book

Time Flies – Where?

We've all been robbed of time. Sometimes the reason for the theft is obvious, other times the reason eludes us, suggesting a problem with deeper roots.

Time cannot be saved. Time must be spent. Since time cannot be saved, what then is the value of time management or event control?

Time-Robbers: Who is robbing us of time? How is the theft taking place?

Time Wasters: Evaluate your own time robbers.

Which time-robbers are causing me to lose control?

TIME ROBBERS

Group A	Group B
Imposed by the environment of your work organization.	Self-Inflicted
Interruptions	Failure to delegate
Waiting for answers	Poor attitude
Unclear job definition	Personal disorganization
Unnecessary meetings	Absentmindedness
Too much work	Failure to listen
Poor Communications	Indecision
Equipment failure	Socializing
Disorganized boss	Fatigue
Shifting priorities	Lack of self-discipline
Red tape/procedures	Leaving tasks unfinished
Understaffed	Paper shuffling
Conflicting priorities	Procrastination

Group A	Group B
Untrained staff	Outside activities
Peer/staff demands	Cluttered workspace
Allowing upward delegation	Unclear personal goals
Inefficient office layout	Perfectionism
Interoffice travel	Poor planning
Mistakes of others	Attempting too much Preoccupation

Controlling Procrastination

What do we lose when we procrastinate? We lose life? We lose opportunity. We lose today.

To the procrastinator, "tomorrow" is a convenient cubbyhole in which to put important tasks.

Procrastinators also suffer in other cruel ways. By waiting for the last minute they often are the one plagued by anxiety and stress.

The procrastinator may even eventually suffer from poor health.

Medical and dental examinations or other necessary visits to the doctor are not pleasant experiences---so appointments never get made. (Which means health slowly deteriorates, and sometimes health issues that are not detected early could have been prevented with just one visit). Therefore we are left with a life-threatening condition.

Other reasons we procrastinate:
1. Over committing, has a paralyzing effect
2. Lack of information
3. Unclear goals
4. Fear of failure
5. Now is not the time
6. General disorganization

AN EVANGELIST SHOULD:

Be Saved

Be Prayerful

Be Studious

Be Neat and Modest Appearance

Be Honest

Be Interested in the welfare of Pastor and Church

Be Alert

Be Thankful

Be Helpful

Be Thrifty

Be Clean and Well-Groomed

Be Punctual

Be Patient

Be Faithful

Be Kind

Be Dignified

Be Spirit Filled

Be a good Representative of Christ

Be a good Representative of the Church and the Department of Evangelism

Be a Man/Woman of Integrity

Does thou love life?

Then do not squander time.

Time is the stuff life is made of.²

²Richard I. Winwood, <u>Time Management</u> (Utah: Franklin International, Inc., 1990) pp. 3, 15-23, 103-105, 110-112, 162

Chapter

3

Job Descriptions for the Local Jurisdiction

❖ **Jurisdictional Evangelist President**

❖ **Jurisdictional Evangelist Vice President**

❖ **Jurisdictional Evangelist Elect Lady**

❖ **Jurisdictional Assistant Elect Lady**

❖ **District Evangelist President**

❖ **District Elect Lady**

❖ **Jurisdictional Executive Secretary**

❖ **Jurisdictional Financial Chairman/Treasurer**

❖ **Local Evangelist President**

❖ **Jurisdictional Evangelist Advisor**

JURISDICTIONAL EVANGELIST PRESIDENT

This is the highest position in the Jurisdictional Evangelist Department. This position should be one of planning and development of projections and instructions handed down from the Jurisdictional Bishop relating to the overall umbrella of Evangelism. This position is responsible for administration of staff members.

RESPONSIBILITIES

1. Presides at all department business meetings.

2. Provide a meeting agenda for meetings and assure that the meetings move expeditiously yet thoroughly. Timeliness must be characteristic of an Evangelist.

3. Responsible for electing or appointing officers and various committee persons to carry out the goals of the department.

4. Must be trained to evangelize – and equipped to train workers.

5. Must be instrumental in keeping the spirit of Evangelism alive.

6. Should help strengthen churches.

7. Should have well-planned Evangelistic program for each Jurisdictional meeting (Spring Worker's Meeting and Convocation) as directed by the Jurisdictional Bishop.

8. Shall have the right to operate within the district with the approval of the District Superintendent and Pastors.

9. Shall lead the Evangelist Department to be an asset to the Jurisdiction.

10. Shall head sectional business meetings with the District Evangelist Presidents.

JURISDICTIONAL EVANGELIST VICE PRESIDENT(S)

The First and Second Vice Presidents of the Evangelist Department may be appointed by the President.

Presides at all department business meetings (in the absence of the President).

Assists the President in the preparation of an agenda for each of the business meetings. Must be trained to evangelize – and equipped to train workers.

Must be instrumental in keeping the spirit of Evangelism alive (lend support to President).

Should help strengthen churches (lend support).

Should have well-planned Evangelist program for each Jurisdictional meeting as directed by the Jurisdictional Bishop (lend support as needed).

Should have the right to operate within the district with the approval of the District Superintendent and Pastors (only in the absence of a President).

Shall lead the Evangelist Department to be an asset to the Jurisdiction (in the absence of a President).

RESPONSIBILITIES

1. Shall contact and develop an on-going relationship with the District Presidents to:

   - See that they are organized.
   - Assure that District Presidents are actively participating in the Jurisdictional Evangelist programs.

2. Should support the Jurisdictional Programs including the Official Day of the President by providing financial support with the help of coordinating the District Presidents.

3. Should work with the Jurisdictional Elect-Lady as she assists the President.

JURISDICTIONAL ELECT LADY

This is the highest position for the female Evangelist Missionaries of the department. The Jurisdictional Elect Lady shall assist the Jurisdictional President in the management of the Jurisdictional Department of Evangelism. This position should be one of planning and development. She oversees the area of Evangelism pertaining to all female Evangelist.

RESPONSIBILITIES

1. Shall assist the Jurisdictional President in the management of the department.

2. Work will include the direction and coordination of District Elect Ladies in their district responsibilities.

3. Will serve on the Jurisdictional Evangelism's Advisory Board and shall be responsible for carrying out the general and national program from the Jurisdictional Supervisor and National Elect Lady.

4. Will recommend Evangelist Missionaries to the department for membership or staff positions deemed necessary within the department.

5. Should be knowledgeable in teaching the Word of God.

6. Shall oversee the workers and delegate authority to the District Elect Ladies and the functions they perform.

7. Performs related duties as required.

JURISDICTIONAL ASSISTANT ELECT LADY

A Right-hand man is a person, male or female, relied upon heavily by another. The term comes from the importance of the right hand in performing tasks (since many people are right-handed). The predominance of right-handedness may account for attitudes of importance and superiority placed on the right over the left by many cultures.

There is speculation that "right-hand male/female" also comes from the idea of a king with his advisor sitting on his right side, by his right hand. However, there is little evidence supporting it.

RESPONSIBILITIES

1.   Shall assist the Jurisdictional Elect Lady in the management of the department.

2.   Shall support the Elect Lady with coordinating the District Elect Ladies in their district responsibilities.

3.   Will serve on the Jurisdictional of Evangelism's Advisory Board.

4.   Will be support to the Elect Lady in the recommendation of Evangelist Missionaries to the Department for membership or staff.

5.   Should be knowledgeable in teaching the Work of God.

6.   Shall support the Elect-Lady in seeing that the District Elect-Ladies understand their function in their District and their responsibility to the Elect-Lady.

7.   Shall support the Elect-Lady financially and encouraging the District Elect-Ladies and all female workers to carry out their responsibility financially.

8.   Performs related duties as required.

DISTRICT EVANGELIST PRESIDENT

RESPONSIBILITIES

1. Must be faithful in their local church with a recommendation from their Pastor and District Superintendent.

2. Must support all District and Jurisdictional Meetings with his presence and finances.

3. Must be willing to assist and support the Jurisdictional Evangelist President and Elect-Lady in conducting crusades in his District.

4. Should help strengthen churches in his District.

5. May conduct a revival in his district at least once a year.

6. Keep a record of all revivals conducted and keep a record of all that were saved.

7. Must be trained to evangelize.

8. Must be instrumental in keeping the spirit of evangelism alive throughout the District.

9. Prepare an Evangelist Institute Hour in the district meetings.

DISTRICT ELECT LADY

RESPONSIBILITIES

1. Must be faithful to their local church with a recommendation from her Pastor and District Superintendent and District Missionary.

2. Must be supportive of all District and Jurisdictional Meetings with her presence and finances.

3. Must assist the District President in preparing the Evangelist Institute Hour in the District meetings.

4. Must support the Jurisdictional Elect-Lady and President.

5. Must be able to train in the area of soul winning.

6. Should conduct revivals and prayer meetings.

JURISDICTIONAL EVANGELIST EXECUTIVE SECRETARY

The secretary is an administrative support position. The title refers to a person who performs routine, administrative, or personal tasks for the Evangelist Department.

RESPONSIBILITIES

1. Coordinate and supervise the work of other clerical personnel and work that may be assigned to the secretary.

2. Must be able to analyze and process administrative reports and perform other related work as required or deemed necessary.

3. Keep the minutes upon request of each business meeting which consist of all the business transactions.

4. Minutes of preceding meeting should be read at all official meetings or upon request by President or Vice-President (provide copies to President, Vice-President, and Elect-Lady prior to meeting).

5. Compose and type forms and/or correspondence from dictation and/or other duties assigned.

6. Maintain a list of members names and addresses, to send to members such notices as the President may require.

7. Greets visitors, arranges appointments and maintains records and files in an orderly and professional manner.

8. Direction as provided in accordance with the Jurisdictional President of Evangelism, Vice-President and Elect-Lady.

9. Performs related work assignments as required.

JURISDICTIONAL FINANCIAL CHAIRMAN/ TREASURER

The Jurisdictional Finance Committee which shall consist of the Jurisdictional Finance Chairman, Evangelist President, Financial Secretary, and Treasurer.

The Treasurer's role is the most important function on the Board, after that of the President. Financial accountability is of the utmost importance to non-profit associations. If you lose faith in your ability to control and account for finances, they lose faith in the whole organization.

RESPONSIBILITIES

1. Carries out the responsibilities of members of the Board of Directors.

2. Assists in the preparation of the department budget.

3. Monitors the budget.

4. Makes sure the Department financial policies are being followed.

5. Handles all receipts and checks for expenditures.

6. Routinely prepares financial reports for the committee and department.

7. Maintains all banking accounts including making bank deposits.

8. Must be able to account for all finances given to them.

As is stated in the job description, the Treasurer is first and foremost a member of the Board. This means that the Treasurer is responsible to the members (as with every Board member) for the funds received and spent by the Department.

The assumption in this job description is that the Treasurer takes a "hands-on" role with respect to the Department. A hands-on Treasurer should go through a monthly routine which would vary depending on the level of involvement. At the very least, a Treasurer should meet with the staff person on a regular basis to go over invoices and checks, to review the bank statements, and to monitor the preparation of monthly statements for the Board.

LOCAL EVANGELIST PRESIDENT

1. Organization should be structured to include an assistant (if possible) and a secretary and workers.

2. Make a list of all workers. The leader's name and position should head the list. Maintain a record of all worker's name, address and telephone number. Make a copy for the District President.

3. Meetings should be held to discuss local projects, district functions and other Evangelist business. Occasionally invite the President and Elect-lady.

4. A meeting agenda should be provided and the meeting should move expeditiously yet thoroughly. Timeliness must be characteristic of an Evangelist.

5. The Local Evangelist should be ready to assist his/her Pastor in prayer, altar work and laying hands on the sick and afflicted.

6. You should be responsible for keeping the spiritual flame burning in the church by conducting prayer meetings and shut-ins.

7. You should encourage, motivate, and stir the congregation to seek more of the Lord.

JURISDICTIONAL EVANGELIST ADVISOR

Goal: To promote the spiritual growth of the Evangelist Department.

Purpose: Assist in the teaching, training, and retraining of new and current Evangelists that come on board throughout the year.

Without counsel purposes are disappointed, but in the multitude of counselors they are established. Proverbs 15:22

Iron sharpeneth iron; so a man sharpeneth the countenance of his friend. Proverbs 27:17

RESPONSIBILITIES

1. Provides information, advice and guidance for Evangelist Department.

2. Promote leadership.

3. Present at all executive meetings with Evangelist Team.

4. Be cognizant of the need to develop relationship with the Evangelist Team.

5. Have a concern for the ongoing functions of the Department.

6. Serving as a resource person as we plan events, programs, and resolving issues.

Chapter

4

Introducing – The Bible to New Converts

❖ **The Bible As The Word of God**

❖ **The Author of the Scriptures**

❖ **How To Study The Scriptures**

INTRODUCING

THE BIBLE TO NEW CONVERTS

THE BIBLE AS THE WORD THE GOD

Lesson 1: Scripture Reference

Jeremiah 36:6 Nehemiah 8:8; Hebrews 1:1,2; John 12:48, 49

1.   <u>A First Purpose in the Study of the Bible.</u>

The reason for knowing the Bible is to come to know God. A good place to begin the study of the Bible is with the first four words: "In the beginning God".

Men have guessed, experimented, pondered, and suggested answers as to the beginning of things, but the Bible uses only four words on the whole matter. It all centers in God. The reason for teaching the Bible to others is that they too may come to know God.

If we come to know only the Book and fail to come to know God through the Book, then we have failed, the Bible has failed in its intent, and God's purpose in the Book has been defeated.

2.   <u>The Author of the Bible.</u>

The word Bible comes from the Greek word *biblos*, which means book. The Bible means The Book. While it contains history, law, biography and poetry, similar in kind to other books, yet it contains something that no other book or group of books claims to contain. It contains within it the Word of the living God. In this it is unique, differing entirely from all others. It is the one and only book of which God can be said to be the author. The abundant proofs of this authorship will be treated in a later study. It is sufficient here to prepare our minds with that degree of reverence and humility which is fitting when we approach the study of a book from the hand of the almighty God.

3.   <u>The Bible is a Holy Book.</u>

The tendency of materialistic times is to make all things carnal and common. Nothing remains as holy or sacred or deserving of reverence. The only change that has taken place however, is in us. There are yet holy things, of which the Bible, containing the Word of God, is one. It calls not only for our study, but also for our reverent study.

4.   <u>The Bible Is God's Voice.</u>

God may reveal Himself to us in many ways, through nature and through the wondrous laws of science, of which He is the author also, yet He speaks to us only through the Bible. Through nature we may come to know him as Creator, but only through the Bible can we hear His voice speaking to us as the Father. It is to learn to hear this "still small voice" that we study the word, observing that His voice is ever attuned to those who would hear, whether in the simple days of the beginnings of spiritual knowledge or in these days of completed revelation.

5. The Bible Is Light.

When we remember that with all the books and all the piled-up knowledge of the world, not one book throws the faintest light into the eternities. We may well appreciate the Bible because it does throw the light much further back than science has ever suggested, and forward into realms where science, by its very nature, can not go. But for that light how very great the darkness would be indeed!

6. The Bible as a Revelation.

The word "revealed" suggests something brought forth that was hidden; something made plain that was obscure; something lighted up that was dark.

God made man in His own image. However, among many other things that may mean, it means that man can think, imagine, dream, and long. He longs to know whence he came, why he is here, and whither he is going. All human knowledge, at its best, throws but little light on any of these subjects. Likewise, man longs to know his Author and what that author's purpose is in him. He wants to know what the future holds. Again human knowledge breaks down.

It is here that the Bible comes to reveal whence man came, what his purpose is, and what the future holds in store. It reveals man to himself and also reveals God to man. Only the Creator could furnish such information; only the Bible contains such information, and hence we speak of the "light of revelation" contained within the Bible.

7. The Bible Is a Divinely Given Guide for Travelers to Eternity.

As a light and as a revelation, the Bible constitutes the only divinely given guide on the pathway of life. Life is short and lived but once. We can not afford to make a mistake. The Author of that Guidebook must be one who knows the whole path and the journey's end. Only one, who sees much farther than any human eye can see, or experience reach, could furnish such a guide. This the heavenly Father has done for us in the Book of books, the Bible.

It is true that the light of this revelation is more like the dim light of the stars as it begins to be shed upon a people just emerging from a state of bondage to a heathen and idol-worshipping nation. Later, through the Word as given by the prophets, it becomes more like the light of the rising full moon, but all was but preparatory for the time when the Sun of Righteousness should arise through whom should be given the full light of day as we have it in the New Testament.

However, for whatever time or people given and however it may be fitted to their capabilities and needs, it yet always, and in all parts, reveals the same loving, patient, kindly, heavenly Father, seeing only to guide, bless, and save.

8.   <u>The Bible as the Word of Truth.</u>

"Know the truth, and the truth shall make you free".   *"Thy word is truth"*.   These two passages suggest a final characteristic of the Bible.   How frankly it recognizes that only by knowledge of the truth can any blessing come!   How blandly the stark truth is related even about its heroes, yet how simply put are the profoundest truths of the universe, such as we find in the first four words of the Bible!

POINTS IN CHRISTIAN PEDAGOGY

(The Art of Teaching)

Some First Qualifications of a Teacher

1. Every teacher of the Bible should be a believer. If he does not know the way, he is unprepared to teach others; if he knows and will not walk therein, he is unworthy to lead.

2. Have a definite purpose in teaching, other than the mere satisfaction of a personal ambition.

3. Understand and try to appreciate the sacredness and tremendous responsibility of handling the Word of God when the souls of men, women, and children are at stake.

4. Be willing to prepare consecrated and painstakingly. The reward is worth much more than all the effort expended.

QUESTIONS ON THE LESSON

1. For what first purpose is the Bible given?

2. In what sense does the literature of the Bible stand entirely along?

3. God being the Author, with what attitude should we approach the study of the Bible?

4. In the light of science, why is the Bible needed?

5. What do we mean by revelation?

6. How do you account for the fact of the clearer more complete revelation of the New Testament since the same God is present in the Old and New Testament?

QUESTIONS ON PEDAGOGY

7. Why must a Bible teacher be a believer?

8. What purpose should guide the teacher?

THE AUTHORITY OF THE SCRIPTURES

LESSON 2:   Scripture References:

Matthew 7:28-29; Mark 1:27
John 5:25-27, Luke 9:1-2
Matthew 28: 18-20

THE LESSON

1.   <u>Necessity for Authority.</u>

In an army there must be authority, else there would be a helpless mob and no army. In a nation there must be authority lodged somewhere. It may be in a constitution made by the people, or elsewhere, but somewhere there must be the source of final appeal, else anarchy and chaos will reign. In a court there must be authority, else no such thing as a court could exist. In that, the law is authority. The judge himself must keep to the law, judge by it and be judged by it.

In religion likewise, there must be authority else there could be no religion. There must be a guide, a source of knowledge, which is final, to which men may go for such guidance, accurate knowledge and final appeal. In the Scriptures rest that authority for Christianity.

2.   <u>Why the Bible is Authoritative.</u>

In our first study we considered the "Bible as the Word of God". Clearly, in matters of religion, there can be no higher authority than the commands of the almighty God. There could be no authority higher and none beyond this, and any below it could not be final. Settle the questions, "Is the Bible the Word of God"? We have settled the questions once and for all as to the scriptures being the authority in religion.

3.   <u>The Scriptures are the Only Authority for Christianity.</u>

There have been other sources of authority suggested and accepted by some. Among these the leading ones are:

1)   The writings of heathen philosophers and sages such as Zoroaster, Confucius, Buddha, Mohammed, and Plato have been upheld as equal authority with the Bible.

2)   The voices of men of genius and the poets such as Shakespeare, Milton and others.

3. The ecclesiastical potentates of the church such as the Pope and Cardinals of Roman Catholicism.

4. The inner consciousness of one's self.

5. Men like Joseph Smith, Alexander Dowie and others of the kind who claimed to be prophets and to receive special revelations from God, in addition to the Bible.

4. Results of Adopting, Additional Authorities.

When we concede to Shakespeare, Confucius, Buddha or Joe Smith, an authority co-equal with the Scriptures, we have simply done away with any final authority. We have destroyed authority by adding authorities. These authorities differ widely. To accept all is to reject all.

Once we let human "inner consciousness" be enthroned as "authoritative" immediately the Bible and God are dethroned. To adopt such, means only complete confusion in religion. To make any human being ecclesiastical or other, an authority, is again to dethrone the Almighty and the Divine and to enthrone the fallible, human mind and word, instead of the mind and Word of the Almighty God.

5. Distinctions of Authority of the Scriptures.

As we shall see in our next studies, not all of the Scriptures are of equal authority in this day.

We shall see that the Scriptures consist of the Old Testament and the new Testament. We live under the New Testament now, and not under the Old. The Old Testament was the authority until fulfilled in Christ and until the New Testament, or complete revelation of God's will, was given. "This will be more clear as we study further".

6. Kinds of Authority.

There are two kinds of authority. There is primary authority such as rests in God. Primary authority rests in our constitution. The constitution delegates or assigns certain authority to our President. He may in turn delegate certain military authority to one whom he appoints as general in chief of the Army. Again he may delegate certain authority to a captain. This is called delegated authority.

Hebrews 1:1-2 suggest primary authority. *Luke 9:1 and Matthew 16:19* suggest delegated authority.

It is made plain in the Bible, however, that though God gave Jesus all authority and He gave certain authority to the apostles; it stops there. Their word is final, and that word we have in the Scriptures, "the faith which was once for all delivered" (*Jude 3*). We can neither add nor take away from God's Word.

7. <u>Summary of Facts of Authority.</u>

We have learned that the authority of the Scriptures rests on the fact that they were produced by inspired men. The writers of the New Testament were directly guided by the Holy Spirit, sent by Christ.

Since God gave Christ all authority and since the Almighty God is the final authority, beyond whom there is and can be none other, we can rest assured that when we have learned the Scriptures we know the will of the one God.

POINTS IN CHRISTIAN PEDAGOGY

Preparation to Teach a Bible Lesson

1. Prepare yourself most thoroughly, not only by study, but also by meditation and prayer. Think of the lesson in terms of the pupils you are to teach. The task is sacred and important enough to call for thorough preparation each time.

2. Determine a main thought, idea or principle to be instilled by means of the lesson, and then prepare to use the lesson to plant that one main thought or idea.

3. Prepare the pupils for the lesson before you begin to teach it. Gain their confidence, friendship and personal regard by your contacts everyday in the week and by your early presence and greeting on Sunday.

4. Prepare your pupils by gaining their interest in the particular lesson that you are going to teach. A few introductory remarks or questions will help to do that. Show a genuine interest yourself.

QUESTIONS ON THE LESSON

1. What is the necessity for authority in religion?

2. Why is the Bible the authority?

3. What other authorities have some adopted?

4. What is the result from adding authorities?

5. What distinction is made as to the authority of the Old and New Testaments today?

6. What do we mean by primary authority and delegated authority? To whom did God and Christ delegate authority?

QUESTIONS ON PEDAGOGY

1. Why the necessity for thorough preparation to teach?

2. How to prepare the lesson?

3. How to prepare the pupils?

4. How to prepare yourself?

LESSON 3:   Scripture Reference:
II Timothy 2:14-21

THE LESSON

Some Fundamental Rules for Studying the Scriptures

1.   <u>A First Rule to Follow</u>

In considering any passage of Scripture, keep carefully in mind the following rule: Determine who is speaking, to whom he is speaking, in what dispensation or for what time he is speaking and for what purpose he is speaking.

It must be kept in mind that while the Scriptures are the Word of God, they also contain, in recorded conversations, histories of events, the words of other inspired men. While the Word is recorded by inspired men, they record, at places, even the words of the devil, or the evil of, misguided or uninformed men.

Also the Word of God has been given to and for three ages: The Patriarchal, the Mosaic and the Christian, in progressive order.

Again, there are Scriptures that are plan instructions for specific times and conditions or for specifically designated men and classes of men. The instructions given to a Christian are not the same as those given to one who has not yet become a Christian.

Examples of the above: *"What have we to do with thee, thòu Son of God"? (Matthew 8:29)*, is a quotation from the devil. *"Whosoever will, let him take the water of life freely" (Revelation 22:17 A.V.)* is a quotation from the apostle John, speaking in the New Testament as the Holy Spirit guides him and speaking to all men everywhere and for all time to come. *"Let us make three tabernacles" (Mark 9:5)*, is a quotation from Peter before he was given the guidance of the Holy Spirit, and was a mistaken suggestion from Peter, immediately corrected by the voice of God. *"And take thou unto thee Aaron thy brother, and his sons with him, from among the children of Israel, that he may minister unto me in the priest's office" (Exodus 28:1 A.V.)*, is a quotation directly from the voice of God, but is quite apparently spoken to a specific person (Moses) and for a specific time, not past.

Even in the writings of the inspired apostle Paul, he makes it plain in a few places that he is there expressing a personal and uninspired opinion, but in all his other writings he makes it plain that he is speaking the Word of the Lord. Keeping the above facts in mind will save us from many an error.

2.   A Second Rule of Importance.

Each Scripture should be interpreted in the light of all other Scriptures. We must know something of that which proceeds and that which follows. For example: In the New Testament conversions, there are found different answers as to what to do to be saved. One is told to believe, another is told to be baptized. There might appear to be confusion. However, when all these passages and other are taken into consideration, the explanation is apparent. Each one was told to take that step which was the next step for him to take in consideration of the steps which he had already taken.

John 3:16 is an example of a well-known Scripture which states a great general truth, but is well understood only when interpreted in the light of other specific things commanded in other passages.

In *Acts 16*, verse 31 needs to be interpreted in the light of the two verses that follow.

3.   Discrimination as to the Testaments.

The word "testament" means, will or covenant. Therefore, New Testament means "new will". We live today under the New Testament, not under the Old. Under the gospel of Christ, not under the Law of Moses. Under the Christian dispensation, not under the Mosaic.

This does not do away with the Old Testament, for it is a book from God as much as is the New. It is the background of the New. It contains the history of the preparation for the New. It helps us understand the divine inspiration of the New. It helps to understand the New, and it contains invaluable lessons in righteousness. Yet know what to do to be saved today, we must go to the New Testament.

"But before faith came, we were kept in ward under the law, shut up unto the faith which should afterwards be revealed. So that the law is become our tutor/schoolmaster to bring us unto Christ, that we might be justified by faith. But now that faith is come, we are no longer under a tutor. *"For ye are all sons of God, through faith in Christ Jesus"* (Galatians 3:23-26).

DIVISIONS AND CLASSIFICATIONS FOR THE SCRIPTURES

1. Natural Divisions of the Books

    As the books of the Bible come in order, they fall not only into the two great divisions, the Old Testament, with it thirty-nine books, and the new Testament, with its twenty-seven books, but there are further divisions according to the purposes of the books.

    As the Bible is to be used by us now, it might be said to consist of five groups of books, as follows: The Old Testament, to lead to the coming of Christ, the Gospels, to reveal Christ to us, that we may believe in Him and want to become Christians; Acts, to tell how to become Christians, the Letters to teach us how to live the Christian life, and Revelation to tell us to be faithful unto death, or, in other words, to keep on living the Christian life to the end.

    This distinction should be kept ever in mind, as it will help us to understand and teach the Word much more clearly. For example, the instructions in the Letters are not to those who have not yet become Christians, but to those who have.

2. A Classification of the Subject Matter of the Scriptures

    Running horizontally through all the books of the Bible, and yet intertwined one with the other, four kinds of Scriptures are easily discernible. All Scriptures consists of: (a) facts to be believed; (b) commands to be obeyed; (c) promises to be received by those who believe the facts and obey the commands; (d) warnings to be heeded by all.

    Sometimes two of these classes of Scripture will appear in a single verse such as *Acts 2:38*: *"Repent ye, and be baptized everyone of you in the name of Jesus Christ unto the remission of sins, and ye shall receive the gift of the Holy Spirit"*. Here a command and a promise appear in the same verse.

3. A Twofold Classification

    Parts of the Scriptures are plain, while other parts seem too deep for comprehension. The explanation is that what man is to do is necessarily plain. God's part in salvation naturally may be beyond our complete comprehension.[3]

[3]Orrin Roots, Training for Service, Revised Version (Ohio: Standard Publishing Co., 1965) p. 3-13

Chapter

5

Messages

❖ **The Mandate of the Evangelist**

❖ **Evangelist, Breaking Out of the Four Walls**

THE MANDATE OF THE EVANGELIST

How is it: That in any 5-block radius we can find a church/storefront and killings, murders and rapes are on the rampage? And on the next morning when we turn on our TV's it's all over the screen.

How is it: That the Word is being preached over the airwaves throughout the week and all day Sunday, and men and women are dying in our streets?

How is it: When the Gospel is so widespread, conventions are taking place all over the world, crusades are going on, revivals are breaking out? (*The harvest is past, the summer is ended, and we are not saved*)

How is it: That the prisons are overflowing with both men and women, and many of them are our children and grandchildren?

How is it: That the AIDS epidemic has overtaken the black population? Where both the young and old alike men and women, boys and girls are infected with this deadly disease and dying by the thousands.

How is it: That the divorce rate among church-folks has reached record high?

How is it: That a gross sin, which provoked God to destroy an entire city, can be named among the people of God. Well God owes Sodom and Gomorrah an apology if noting be done about the laws of marriages that are being passed in the legislator?

How is it: That men and women can preach on Sunday morning, until little demons tremble and on Monday live lives of reproach?

Lastly, how is it: That our love ones lay hopelessly and helplessly in the hospital, sick unto death, when we as believers have been given the power and authority to lay hands on the sick and they recover?

Time will not allow me to bring up the varies maladies of our day, such as:

- Teenage pregnancy
- Teenage runaways
- Domestic Violence
- Homelessness
- Homosexuality
- Lesbianism
- War in the Middle East
- Terrorism
- Greed in society and in the church
- Corruption in high places
- Black on Black crimes
- Drugs in our neighborhood

ALARMING FACTS
Let's look at a few statistics of our day.

Divorce

Half of the children (in the United States) will witness the breakup of a parent's marriage. Of these, close to half will also see the breakup of a parent's second marriage.

Christians are more likely than non-Christians to experience divorce. (Among Christians, 27% report they've gone through a divorce, only 25% of non-Christians report that they have).

Divorce in America is a $28 billion-a-year industry.

Since 1972, millions of children each year have lived through the divorce of their parents.

Studies in the early 1980s showed that children in repeat divorces earn lower grades and their peers rated them as less pleasant to be around.

Sixty percent of black women who married in the 1960s and early 1970s had already experienced a divorced by 1992.

Forty percent of divorced children growing up in America have tripled since 1980.

HIV/AIDS among African Americans

The HIV/AIDS epidemic is a major health crisis among African Americans, affecting men and women of every age and sexual orientation.

Across every measure, African Americans account for a disproportionate share of AIDS cases in the United States. The statistics that I will present indicate a problem so severe, some believe Black America is in a "State of Emergency". Unless action is taken to stem the incidents of AIDS cases among black males, women and children, this growing crisis will soon overwhelm our nation's healthcare system and may derail our national prosperity.

1. Blacks make up 13% of the United States population, but 47% of the AIDS cases in the Nation.

2. Nationally, the number of AIDS cases per 100,000 is nearly 10 times higher for blacks as it is for whites; 76.8 for blacks but only 8.1 for whites.

3. AIDS is the leading cause of death for African Americans between the ages of 25 and 44.

4. AIDS cases among black males is 7 times the rate for white males.

5. Black women make up 63% of the AIDS cases among women nationwide.

6. The rate of AIDS cases among black women is 23 times the rate of white women. Why are women at greater risk both educated women and women with only a high school education. Again, why is this? I will only share one reason, and that is, women that are in relationships with men that are in bi-sexual relationships with other men who are secretly engaging in high-risk behaviors such as having unprotected sex with men. Saints we must educate our children and ourselves.

7. In 2000, 64% of all the AIDS cases reported among young people ages 13 to 19 were black.

8. The rate of AIDS cases among black children under the age 13, is 23 times higher than the rate for white children.

Blacks in Prison

More blacks in prison than in College:

In 1997 of the 8,070,225 total arrest nationwide, 2,675,786 were black Americans.

Black men are more likely than white men to be imprisoned during their lifetime.

Another Department of Justice statistic show black males 10 times more likely to enter State or Federal prison before age 20 than whites of similar age. And a shocking 21.4 percent of black males will be incarcerated by age 30 versus 1.4 percent of while males.

The explosion in the African American prison and jail populations has had a devastating and alarming impact on the black communities across the nation. Incarcerating black men between ages of 16 and 34, in the prime of their lives, leads to several negative consequences, which reduces their opportunity to ever enter the labor market given a prison record.

It has been argued that a decline in the African American "male marriage-eligible pool" has caused an increase in out-of-wedlock births in the black community. They contend that high unemployment, mortality, and incarceration among young African American males have reduced the ration of marriage-eligible black males black females. Ex-convicts are less attractive as marriage partners or as fathers, thereby negatively affecting family structure.

Many Black men with prison records are virtually unemployable, poor marriage partners and therefore unlikely to reintegrate into the community. The young children of these men are at risk to continue the tragic legacy of their fathers.[4]

The Bible's Answer to Motivate Evangelism

We are faced with a dilemma as Jeremiah was. I would like to ask all of you a question. How shall we escape, if we neglect so great of salvation? Jeremiah questions the illness of his day.

"Is there no balm in Gilead? Is there no physician there? Why then has not the health of the daughters of my people been restored"?

Balm was highly esteemed and the leaders of that day believed that it would completely restore a man to vibrant and vigorous activities. If balm was given in Canary wine, every morning it would renew youth, strengthen the brain, relieve languishing nature and prevent baldness. Balm is sovereign for the brain, strengthening the memory and powerfully chasing away depression. How many of you would pay good money for this Balm? Balm is a medicine salve. The people were wounded from their sins with idolatries and needed to be restored.

After the captivity, when Israel took the Promised Land, Gilead, on the West Side of the Jordan became part of their land. The tribe of Gad settled there. The balm trade then became one with Israel. The reason for all this was that of there secreted-turpentine like adhesive substance by some plant that was highly sought after. It is said that this balm was worth twice its weight in silver.

So, Jeremiah's question is, "How can a people who traded in balm be so sick". Of course there is a weightier question to illustrate a spiritual point. How can the people of God, with the law in their midst, be so sinful? Let's bring it closer to home, how can the people of God have the Gospel and chose darkens over light.

In Jeremiah's day there was not a man to be found.

Jeremiah 5:1 – "Run ye to and from through the streets of Jerusalem, and see now, and know, and seek in the broad places thereof, if ye can find a man, if there be any that executeth judgment, that seeketh the truth; and I will pardon it".

God bids them search the town, look in the streets. Is there a man that is truly conscientious, and will speak the truth, yet you shall not find in the streets and broad places, he dare not appear publicly, lest he should be abused and run down. Truth is fallen in the street, and is forced to seek for corners.

Out of all the warning and corrections they were given, they still refuse to receive correction. They have made their faces harder than a rock.

What was the solution for the Jews? What is our solution today? It was simply use the balm that they already had. For the believers it is receive the Gospel.

Today, there is a tendency as believers to look upon what the children of Israel did and shake our heads in disbelief, tempted to say, "I'm, glad we've learned our lesson and will go to God for what we need". But are we doing this on a daily basis, are we doing this when the going gets tough and the tough gets going. Can we stand and as Job did and say, *"Though he slay me, yet will I trust him, "*. *Job 18:15*

Let's consider the state of the Church in Laodicea: they said: *"Because thou sayest, I am rich and increased with goods; and have need of nothing, and knowest not that thou are wretched, and miserable, and poor, and blind, and naked; I counsel thee to buy of me gold tried in the fire, that thou mayest be rich; and white raiment, that thou mayest be clothed, and that the shame of thy nakedness do not appear; and anoint thine eyes with eye salve, that thou mayest see".* *Revelations 3:18*

In great parallel to ancient Israel and the balm of Gilead, Laodicea was only 13 miles away from a school famous for its medical knowledge, particularly it's eye salve. And yet they were blind.

Because of the condition of the people, Jeremiah refused to be comforted. What caused such heartache? *Jeremiah 8:21-23 "It is for the hurt of the daughter of my people, that I am hurt, it is for their sin, and the miseries they have brought upon themselves by it, it is for this that I am black, that I look black. That I go in black as mourners do. And that astonishment has taken hold on me, so that I know not what to do or which way to turn.*

Is there no balm in Gilead? No medicine proper for a sick and dying kingdom? Is there no physician there, no skillful faithful hand to apply the medicine? He looks upon the case to be deplorable and past relief. There is no balm in Gilead that can cure the disease of sin, no physician there that can restore the health of a nation quite overrun by such a foreign arm as that of the Chaldeans.

The desolations made are irreparable, and the disease has presently come to such a height that there is no curing of it.

Is there no balm in Gilead, no physician there? Yes, certainly there is. God is able to help and heal them. There is a sufficiency in him to redress all their grievances.

Why then was not their health restored? The failure was not in God, but to themselves. It was not for want of balm and a physician, nor is it because the Gospel has not been preached over the world. But because they would not admit the application nor submit to the methods of cure. The physician was ready, but the patient was willful and irregular, would not adhere to the warning.

It is not only possible but God's desire is that men would be saved and none be lost. When believers cry out to God in true repentance, he is committed to hear and forgive them.

"If I shut up heaven that there be no rain, or if I command the locust to devour the land, or if I send pestilence among my people"; If my people, which are called by my name, shall humble themselves, and pray, and seek my face, and turn from their wicked ways; then will I hear from heaven, and will forgive their sin, and will heal their land". II Chronicles 7:13-14

EVANGELIST, BREAKING OUT OF THE FOUR WALLS
Acts 8:26-40

A Burger King by my house just went out of business. Every time I went in there, the people behind the counter were rude and pre-occupied with their own business. Many times as I was trying to order my combo #3 with no pickles. The cashier would go and start arguing with the "fry guy". Often customers would be waiting for service while the manager in the back was trying to resolve the most recent scheduling problems, or employee conflict. Well, it wasn't long before they were out of business.

I'll bet all of us know why? Ask me? They forgot what they were there for. They forgot that the whole reason that a fast chain exists isn't to be concerned about what's going on behind the counter. The whole reason they exist is to provide food for the people at the drive through or on the other side of the counter and provide it fast.

Unfortunately, that can be true of the church today. It is possible that we can get so caught up with what's going on inside the church walls, shepherding our own people, another building fund, choir day, afternoon social, a baby contest, a convention here a seminar there, that we forget the people outside that are lost. We forget the main reasons we still exist in this world on this corner and that is to "go and make disciples (learners) of all nations" (different governments)

When I think of the word forget, the following comes to mind: (to lose the remembrance of, fail to remember or recall, ignore, put out of the mind). Briefly, let's look at the solemn warning God gave to his people.

> ***Deuteronomy 6:10-12***: *And it shall be, when the Lord thy God shall have brought thee into the land which he swear unto they fathers, to Abraham, to Isaac, and to Jacob, to give thee great and goodly cities, which thou buildedst not, and houses full of all things, which thou filledest not, and wells digged, which thou diggedest not, vineyards and olive trees, which thou plantedst not, when thou shalt have eaten and be full, then beware lest thou forget the Lord, which brought thee forth out of the land of Egypt, from the house of bondage.*

> ***Romans 1:24-32***: *Because that when they knew God they glorified him not as God, neither were thankful, but became vain in their imaginations, and their foolish heart was darkened.*

> *Professing themselves to be wise, they became fools. And changed the glory of the incorruptible God into an image made like to corruptible man, and to birds, and four-footed beasts, and creeping things.*

> *Wherefore God also gave them up to uncleanness through the lust of their own hears, to dishonor their own bodies between themselves.*

Who changed the truth of God into a lie, and worshipped and served the creature more than the Creator, who is blessed forever.

For this cause God gave them up unto vile affections, even their women did change the natural use into that which is against nature.

And likewise also the men, leaving the natural use of the woman, burned in their lust one toward another, men with men working that which is unseemly, and receiving in themselves that recompense of their error which was meet.

And even as they did not like to retain God in their knowledge, God gave them over to a reprobate mind, to do those things which are not convenient.

Being over a period of time filled with all unrighteousness, maliciousness, full of envy, murder, debate, deceit, malignity, whispers.

Backbiters, hater of God, despiteful, proud, boasters, inventors of evil things, disobedient to parents. Without understanding, covenant-breakers, without natural affections, implacable, unmerciful.

Who knowing the judgment of God, that they which commit such things are worthy of death, not only do the same, but have pleasure in them that do them.

So how do we reach those who aren't coming into the walls of our churches? How do we reach the "Unchurched"? Or more specifically, how do we reach the "Unchurched Teens"?

If we are not disturbed (alarmed, made uneasy) with the many lost teens in our world, Lord Help Us!

There are four essentials in reaching the "Unchurched Teen":

1.   *Stay Current* – If we are going to reach the "Unchurched" we need to know what students are going through. We must be aware of what students are watching, listening to, struggling with, and being surrounded with.

2.   *Stay Connected* – The best way to stay current is to get connected with unchurched students. We get connected by going where the unchurched are. Have we allowed ourselves to be to busy with our own children to go to football games, help a little league coaching, be on campus yard duty, visit teens in prisons, go to children's class rooms.

3.   *Stay Creative* – Creative programming, events discussions, and teaching can make or break an outreach ministry. How are they going to hear the Gospel if we can't even get their attention? Are we saying, "this is the way we've always done it".

4.   *Stay Clean* – An example of loving teens doesn't mean digressing to their level, it means loving them for who they are, and loving them enough not to let them stay comfortable in

sin. How can we give an answer to a teen or our own children if they see us fighting, see us talking about one another. See us living one life at church and an entirely different life at home.

I believe it's time for the church (members of the body) to go outside the four walls of the church and do what Jesus has commanded us to do.

Matthew 28:19: *"Go therefore and make disciples (learners) of all the nations (different governments), baptizing them in the name of the Father and of the Son and of the Holy Spirit, teaching them to observe all things that I have commanded you; and lo, I am with you always, even to the end of the age".*

It's time for the church to take Jesus to the streets. It's time to stir ourselves up in the Holy Ghost and do what we have been created to do. It's time to break off complacency and get out of our comfort zones. It's time for us to work the works of God while it is day, for when night comes no make can work.

If you were given $86,400.00 today what would you spend it on? What if I gave that to you every day for the rest of the year, could you spend it? I'll give you a minute to think about it.

There are 86,400 seconds in a day. How are you spending this time?

Count with me up to 20, there's someone dying every second.

Again, how are you spending your time telling the lost about Jesus? Remember, money like time after it is spent, you can never get it back.

How many times have we heard growing up, Jesus is coming soon. Time is running out. These are the last days. (Whew)

Similar words were spoken in Noah's day, It's gonna rain. These words rang 120 years and men's heart and mind became dull because of the repetitive message and the hardness of their heart.

Unfortunately, many today will be caught up in this prophesy.

Evangelist, the World Is Our Field

The world was Phillip's field – and he went.
Acts 8:26-40

How many people make up society?

How many in this society belong to somebody's church?

How many have stop going to church altogether?

Let's take a look. The Census Bureau today projected that on January 1, 2006 the United States population was 297,821,175 up to 2,713,548 or 0.9% from New Year's Day 2005.

In January, the United States is expected to register one birth every eight seconds and one death every 12 seconds.

At approximately 10:34 on November 30, 2005 it was reported that there are 6,560,282,895 billion people in the entire world, and in the United States the count was at 300,314,189 million people. At every eight seconds the number is going steadily up. And of course, we must subtract the death rate and still the population is alarming. Alarming compared to the number of lost souls.

Now that we have seen a glimpse of the number of people in the world, how many are attending are not attending someone's church? It is estimated that there are over 140-160 million unchurched people in America. We lose 72 churches per week or 10.2 per day. We gain 24 churches per week 3.5 per day.

On the average, evangelical churches younger than 3 years old, annually win 10 people to Christ per 100 church members. Those 3-15 years old, win 5 people to Christ. Those older than 15 years old annually win 3 people to Christ. This is not people joining the church today and gone after a month.

Half of all churches last year did not add one new member through "conversion growth".

Fact: North America is the only continent where Christianity is not growing. Churches in America are losing 2,765,000 members per year. Two out of every three Americans are lost. While the population of the United States grows, between 3,500 and 4,000 churches in the United States die each year?

It is estimated that only 30% of black Americans have been evangelized while 50% of White Americans have been evangelized. It is estimated that 53,000 people in the United States leave churches every week and never come back.

If it is not time that we as Evangelists don't come out of our ceiled houses; then who will win the vast number of lost that we have been commissioned to reach. Please keep in mind these statistics change daily, but they are not far off.

I have heard that God is moving mightily in Third World Countries. People are going to church and walking for miles, 20,000, 30,000 and even higher at various settings. They are glad and excited to go and worship. They don't have fancy cars, fancy clothes, and fancy homes. They are coming with nothing to receive something from God.

On the average, some of us have two cars, but will not come to church only until a disaster strikes, such as 9-11, or some type of tragedy. Forget about the weekly services. We can close our eyes if we want to, but look around.

Have things become to easy for us? Have we gotten careless with our salvation? If we are slow, indifferent, and careless with our own salvation, how will we come to grips with lost sinners?

My questions is, do we really believe that God is on his way back?

Maybe there have not been enough disappointments, maybe the government have not failed us often enough for us to be shakened and seek God. Maybe, the price of gas is still affordable for us to pay.

What will it take for us to GO!

Question: How much are we indebted to a dying world? How far are we willing to go?

Here we see the success and progress of Phillip, not Phillip the apostle, but Phillip the deacon who was chosen and ordained to serve tables. Faithfully working in the office of a deacon now able to move forward in great boldness and faith.

Note: What is your assignment?

Stephen was advanced to the degree of a Martyr, and Phillip to the degree of an Evangelist.

Where has God placed you and have you saturated (soaked) yourself in the word of God and in prayer?

Evangelist, if we have not prepared ourselves for the first assignment, God cannot and will not allow us to go to the next one. (If we are not faithful over a few things, we will never be ruler of the many).

There is a tendency for Evangelist to successfully complete an assignment and get stuck (excited) with their stay.

Evangelist where do you see yourself in the next year? Where is the Lord directing you? Personally I want to go to Israel, I want to go to Africa, I want my feet to touch foreign soil, I want to learn another language and minister to others near and far.

There is no group people, no race, creed or nationality that God's word is not meant to reach. Which tells me I must be sensitive to the directing of the Holy Spirit to go where God sends me. Did Phillip preach his own agenda?

Let's think about this:. Why do people become unchurched? The church needs to give more robust defense of the reason for believing. People pleaded for the churches to answer the skeptics and defend the faith. Respondents wanted evidence for their faith and teaching that upheld the authority of the Bible.

The second reason for delusion was frustration with church leader's not teaching holiness of God and moral standards.

A lot of pastor's and church workers would be surprised to learn that people are leaving churches because they do not defend the faith well enough.

It is sad to believe that what people are looking for is stricter moral teachings. The city of Nineveh needed to hear the words Repent. *Jonah 3:1-10.*

Again, did Phillip have his own agenda? It seems that Phillip would have objected to leaving the great success of the work in Samaria to go out to the desolate desert, but God had a plan for one man. Some boy, some girl, some women and some man is waiting for you and me. They will never step their foot in a church building. Will you go out to them?

Phillip did not preach denomination, the latest trends and fashion to stay away from, or to conform to, the stock market, race, social politics or church politics. He preached Christ.

We often shrink back from speaking boldly about Jesus, in fear of being talked about. Think about it, does the world shrink back from cramming its junk down our throats?

God had arranged this meeting between Phillip and the Ethiopian. This is a glorious example of how God opens doors for Evangelism. God wouldn't have directed Phillip unless God had already arranged an open door. Our greatest challenge in preaching the gospel is praying for open doors, and keeping alert to opportunities God presents to us.

Evangelists we must know, that the mandate God has given to us supersedes, our money, our thoughts, our material possession, our feeling, our disappointments, or gain and our loss. When the Holy Spirit prompts me to move, I must submit to his voice and say yes Lord. Where you lead me I will follow.

The world like the Ethiopian does not understand the things of God unless we share the good news with them. How can I understand unless someone guide me? The plea for a lost world. If there is no understanding of who God is, what he came for, there will never be believers. How can you believe something you don't understand. To get anything from our Bibles, we must plunge in. Butterflies wander over the flowers in the garden and accomplish nothing. But bees plunge right down into the flower, and carry away essential food. We won't get anything if we just hover over our Bibles. We have to dive right in.

Chapter

6

The Do's and Don'ts for the Evangelist

❖**What an Evangelist Should Do**

❖**What an Evangelist Should Not Do**

WHAT AN EVANGELIST SHOULD DO

The Do's

1. Clearly understand the real purpose the Pastor had in mind when he accepted your services to his church. (Gave you the appointment).

2. Do the best job you can to serve in the area of Evangelism in which you agreed to minister in.

3. Always remember you are there to:

   ❗ Win Souls

   ❗ Help the church in one or more of the following ways:
   Spiritually
   Numerically
   Financially
   Educationally

4. Help the Pastor. There are many ways a good Evangelist can help a Pastor whether or not he is having problems in his church. (Ask an experienced Evangelist or the National President).

5. An Evangelist's role, especially in and around the church or in the home of the Pastor or the home of church members, should be beyond reproach. Sir, be a gentlemen, be a Saint. Madame, be a real lady, be a Saint.

6. Liberality, is a distinct virtue of Evangelists. There is much truth to the old saying "It takes money to make money". A stingy Evangelist will never get very far. He must show the people he is willing to lead the way in blessing both the church and Pastor. His reward for doing so is usually abundant.

7. Pay all personal bills or debts you have made during your stay before leaving town or the church. Yes, leave no unpaid debts. This has been a killer to many Evangelists.

8. Be Prayerful. A prayerful life is extremely important for any laborer in Christ.

9. Read and Study. A well read person in any walk of life is usually exciting at all times with thoughts, ideas and newly acquired knowledge. The constant study of the Word of God is a paramount for enlightenment in scriptural truth and is the real life of an Evangelist.

   "Study to shew thyself approved unto God, a workman that needeth not be ashamed, rightly dividing the word of truth." II Timothy 2:15

10. Be a business man or woman. The spiritual spectrum should always be number one in Evangelism; always remember this. Evangelism is big business and you should never forget that an agreeable business side plays an important role in having a smoothly operated meeting. It is ideal to have a good understanding with the Pastor (or proper officials, if there's no Pastor) about the financial program.

11. Preach/deliver the Word and Minister to the needs of the people. Do your homework as to the people that you are going to be ministering to. Don't be a lazy Evangelist.

An Evangelist Should:

Be Saved

Be Prayerful

Be Studious

Be Neat and Modest Appearance

Be Honest

Be Interested in the welfare of Pastor and Church

Be Alert

Be Thankful

Be Helpful

Be Thrifty

Be Clean and Well-Groomed

Be Punctual

Be Patient

Be Faithful

Be Kind

Be Dignified

Be Spirit Filled

Be a good Representative of Christ

Be a good Representative of the Church and the Department of Evangelism

Be a Man/Woman of Integrity

WHAT AN EVANGELIST SHOULD NOT DO

The Don'ts

1. Don't seek out and/or prey upon the weaknesses of the church where you're serving.

2. Don't listen to or accept anything told you against the Pastor or any member.

3. Don't join in with any group or member against the Pastor nor his program.

4. Don't ever exert any effort to prove you're a better preacher or administrator than the Pastor.

5. Don't try to set the church in order.

6. Don't be an excessive burden in a home or to the church in any way.

7. Don't just be interested in money.

8. Don't be a lazy Evangelist. It's alright to offer to be of assistance in little things where you're staying or in the church.

9. Don't expect the money to come automatically because you're there. You have to work for it. Preach and minister.

10. Don't borrow money from members of the church where you serve.

11. Don't try to prove how late you can hold the congregation.

12. Don't leave unpaid telephone bills or other bills where you were a guest.

13. Don't collect the members addresses so you can write them to send you their tithes and financial support after you have left the church or town. Their tithes and support belongs to the home church.

14. Don't preach healing and fail to preach Salvation through Christ.

15. Don't overstay your time. It's always best to leave while the people yet enjoy you. You'll be welcomed back.

16. Don't wear out your welcome. Never try to go to a church too often and don't stay too long, simply because the Pastor accepts you and it's a good financial spot. You will lose the respect of the people and the Pastor.

Chapter 7

How to Be a Witnessing Church

❖ **Personal Evangelism**

❖ **Prayer Follow-Up Card**

❖ **Hints for the Street Evangelist**

❖ **Helps in Witnessing**

❖ **Helpful Reminders**

❖ **Objections and Excuses**

Phase I - Seven Steps to the Kingdom

This is a person-to-person evangelism and we use a system called "Steps to the Kingdom". The approach is precise and can be completed in a minute's time. The approach is to get a verbal agreement with a candidate for one minute of their time. Upon agreement for the one minute, we state that Jesus Christ is Lord and that He loves the candidate. We encourage them to confess Jesus Christ is Lord according to *Romans 10:9*. We proceed to have them pray the prayer of salvation. After the prayer, if they confess that the Lord Jesus Christ is in their heart, our mission is complete. We ask the candidate for information by which we can follow up on them at a later date.

This approach can be done almost anywhere and in a short amount of time a seed has been planted.

1. **Greeting**: (Get a verbal contact) *"Hello, may I have one minute of your time?"*

2. **State**: "Did you know that Jesus Christ is Lord? Well He is and He loves you and wants to be your Lord and Savior."

3. **Say**: Romans 10:9 says, *"If you confess with your mouth the Lord Jesus and believe in your heart that God raised Jesus from the dead, you shall be saved."* Do you believe that?

4. **Ask**: "Can you say Lord Jesus?" (This step brings in the presence of the Holy Spirit.)

5. **Pray**: Reach out for the candidate's hand and say, "Let's pray. Repeat after me:"

> "Lord Jesus, forgive me for all my sins. I repent from my ways. Wash me in your blood and cleanse me from all unrighteousness. I believe that you died on the cross, were buried, and on the third day, God the Father raised you from the dead. Right now, Lord Jesus, I open the door to my heart and I receive you into my heart as my Lord and personal Savior."

6. **The Question**: Say to the candidate: *According to the prayer you just prayed, where is the Lord Jesus now?* The response should be, "He's in my heart." If some other statement is given, repeat Step 5.

7. **Confirmation**: When the candidate gives the correct answer, share with them I John 4:4, *Greater is He that is in you than he that is in the world.* Leave them with a tract. Get their name, address and telephone number for follow-up.

Phase II - S.W.A.T. (Soul Winning Across Town) Team

The SWAT Team is a group evangelism effort that is organized in the church. Members of the congregation break up into teams of three. Each team has a captain. This person should be proficient in performing the witnessing approach (7 Steps to the Kingdom).

Next, a section of the community is mapped out and streets designated for house-to-house or door-to-door evangelism. There are usually two teams assigned per street (a team on each side of the street).

Teams are prayed over and sent out for approximately one hour. As the teams go from door-to-door on the assigned street, each candidate who prays the prayer for salvation is given a tract, a schedule of church services and invited to the next church service. The team will record that person's name, address, and phone number for later follow up. These records are turned into a central location when the teams return to the church.

Phase III - Apollos Ministry

The Apollos Ministry is the watering of the seeds that have been planted during witnessing. The Apollos Ministry is responsible for placing a call to all who prayed the prayer for salvation. The call should be made within 48 hours. The Apollos minister will reiterate the plan of salvation, inquire if there are any special needs to be prayed for, invite the convert to the next church service, offer transportation service (if it is available), and let the convert know they will meet them personally in the church lobby.

The Apollos Ministry will also follow up by sending a card one week and a letter the next week and then another call. The follow up is continued until the convert gives one of the following responses: 1) I have another church I am attending; 2) I am attending your church services; or 3) I no longer wish to be contacted.

PRAYER FOLLOW-UP CARD

Name:_____

Address:_____

**Telephone No.: (_____)_____

E-Mail Address _____

Best time to call: _____AM or _____PM

List names of others in household who said "Sinners Prayer":
(If youth under age 15, please include age)

1._____   4._____

2._____   5._____

3._____   6._____

Total Count in Household: _____

Date:_____   **Team Captain:**_____

                                Team Members:_____

                                _____

                                _____

HINTS FOR THE STREET EVANGELIST

1. Choose a target

2. Determine measurable goals

3. Have a plan of action to accomplish these goals

4. People that do street evangelism must be spiritually prepared and prayed up

5. Workers must have a "stick-to-it" attitude

6. Have appropriate literature

7. Workers must know something about the area they are working and people's lifestyle

8. Workers should be able to look beyond surface problems and circumstances

9. Workers should use plenty of Spirit filled common sense

10. Don't wear jewelry or carry big pocketbooks or large amounts of money

11. Dress moderately

12. Stay away from lengthy discussion on "superficial: issues such as smoking, drinking, which church is the true church, etc.

13. Don't approach those that are with a group getting high

14. Avoid all groups where they are doing something negative or rowdy

15. Avoid dealing with the opposite sex

16. Workers must be in groups of two's

17. Avoid confrontations if at all possible

18. Don't take any threats lightly

19. If they react negatively to the Gospel, be ready to suffer the consequences

20. Don't place your hands on anyone's head

21. Keep your prayers short

22. Never look down on people

23. Encourage people. Bring hope to them. You don't have to focus on their sin. They are well aware of their sin.

HELPS IN WITNESSING

If you thoroughly examine the subjects and memorize the Scriptures, you will find frequent use of this material.

Afflictions

Are often providential   *Psalms 119:67, 71-75*
God will deliver   *Psalms 34:19*

Anxiety

Is relieved through prayer   *Philippians 4:6-7*
Remember God care for your   *1 Peter 5:7*

Assurance

Eternal life promised   *John 3:16*
You can be sure   *1 John 5:11-13*

Comfort

Jesus the Good Shepherd   *Psalms 23*
He will never forsake you   *Hebrews 13:5-6*

Discouragement

Don't give up   *Galatians 6:9*
God will help and strengthen   *Isaiah 41:10*

Emptiness

Christ can satisfy   *Psalms 107:8-9*
He will fulfill your desires   *Psalms 37:4-5*

Forgiveness

Forgiveness and cleansing promised   *Psalms 32:5; 1 John 1:9*

Guilt

No condemnation   *Romans 8:1*
No sin too great   *Isaiah 1:18*

Judgment

Everyone accountable *Romans 14:12; Hebrews 9:27*

Loneliness

His presence promised *Hebrews 13:5-6*
In His presence is joy *Psalms 16:11*

Suffering

Suffering has profit *Hebrews 12:6-11*
It deepens the faith *1 Peter 1:6-7*
It's to be expected *1 Peter 2:19-23*
God's grace is sufficient *II Corinthians 12:9-10*

Temptations

How to avoid them *Matthew 26:41*
What causes failure *James 1:13-14*

Victory

Is in Christ *Philippians 4:13*
Your inner resource *1 John 4:4*
Seek God's help *1 Corinthians 10:13*

Worry

God will provide *Philippians 4:19*
Have faith in Him *Romans 4:20-21*
Claim His promise *I John 5:14-15*

HELPFUL REMINDERS

✓ Do use your Bible (*Psalms 19:7*). Don't present your own ideas.

✓ Do use your Bible as a sword (*Ephesians 6:17*). Don't use it as a club (*Ephesians 4:15*).

✓ Do encourage response. Don't force a decision.

✓ Do ask questions. Don't take anything for granted.

✓ Do be a good listener. Don't do all the talking (*Proverbs 18:13*).

✓ Do be polite. Don't argue *(II Timothy 2:24)*

✓ Do be positive and show that they gain through Christ. Don't overemphasize the negative.

✓ Do be interested in them. Don't pry into their affairs.

✓ Do be friendly. Don't be familiar.

✓ Do be considerate. Don't delay unnecessarily.

✓ Do speak as an equal and identify with the person.. Don't preach.

✓ Do be kind. Don't run down another's faith or denomination.

✓ Do be brief and simple. Don't try to give them a full Bible course.

✓ Do keep faith with the inquirer. Don't betray their confidence.

✓ Do be pleasant and smile. Don't scowl.

OBJECTIONS AND EXCUSES

I'm too Bad	*Hebrews 7:25*
	Isaiah 1:18
There's too much to give up	*Mark 8:36*
	I John 2:15-17
I'm afraid I couldn't hold out	*I Peter 1:5*
	Philippians 1:6
I'm afraid of what others might think	*Matthew 10:32-33*
Not now, some other time	*Proverbs 27:1*
I'm doing the best I can	*Ephesians 2:8-9*
	Isaiah 64:6
I'm not so bad	*James 2:10*
	Isaiah 53:6
God will not condemn anyone	*John 3:18-36*
	Hebrews 9:27
How do I know that God will accept me?	*John 6:37*
	II Peter 3:9
I can't understand the Bible	*I Corinthians 2:14*
	II Corinthians 5:7
How do I know that Christ is the only way?	*John 14:6*
	Acts 4:12
I'd rather have my fun now	*Ecclesiastes 11:9*
	II Corinthians 6:2
Following Christ cost too much	*Mark 8:36*
	Luke 18:29-30
Jesus wasn't really God	*Hebrews 1:3*
	John 10:30
It doesn't sound reasonable	*Isaiah 55:8-9*
	I Corinthians 1:18-23
I'll take my chances	*Hebrews 10:31*
	Luke 12:16-21
I don't believe in Christ	*Romans 3:3*
	Acts 4:12

BIBLIOGRAPHY

Richard I. Winwood, Time Management, Salt Lake City, Utah
Franklin International Inc.

Orrin Roots, Training for Service, Revised Version, Cincinnati, Ohio
Standard Publishing Co.

Thompson Chain-Reference Study Bible, King James Version
World Bible Publishers, Inc.
Iowa falls, IA 50126 U.S.A

Clarence Larkin, Dispensational Truth,
Rev. Clarence Larkin Est.
Glenside, PA 19038 U.S.A

National Statistics – Source: Bureau of Justice Statistics as of June 30, 2003

Jon Cohen – Slate Magazine - A Silent Epidemic – AIDS,
Medical Examiner

Jonathan McKee, The source for Youth Ministry

U.S. Census Bureau – U.S. POPClock Projection

www.civicenterprises.net/pdfs/thesilentepidemic3-06.pdf -

http://groups.com/group/att.activism.death-peanlty/msg/088F6d30dc2dGF90?h1=en&PeterWebb; .Why Are So Many Black Men In Prison," Nov. 2006

http://www.wayoflifeorg.fbis/subscripe.htm. - Divorce Is Rampant Among Christian Leaders

http://www.cpyu.org – Outreach and Evangelism Toady – Epic Evangelism